Hebrew Reading Adventure

אָלֶף-בֵּית Review

Here are all the Hebrew letters in order. Review them by saying the name of the letter and its sound.

.1   א ב ב ג ד ה ה ו ז ח ט י

.2   כ כ ך ל מ ם נ ן ס ע

.3   פ פ ף צ ץ ק ר שׁ שׁ ת

Here are the Hebrew letters again but this time they are out of order. Say the sound of each letter.

.4   פ ל ב ע ד

.5   שׁ א ד ם ט

.6   י ר פ ז נ ו

.7   ב ה ק כ ת

.8   מ צ ח ג ן

.9   שׁ ס ץ פ כ

Match the Hebrew letter with its English name.

Mem
Kaf
Ayin
Tav
Gimmel
Shin
Dalet
Bet

4

You are standing at the edge of a steep cliff. Down below, you see a small siddur fragment that Deke Duke dropped. You eye the cliff and realize that if you are careful you can climb down to safety. But wait! Some footholds are missing. Fill in the missing letters and use them and a rope to climb down safely.

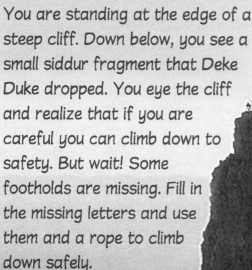

Whew! You reach the bottom safely. You grab the scrap from the siddur but some of the letters are faded. You look back to the mountain for clues. Write the matching letters in each shape you will be able to make out the word.

Go to page 31 and fill in these same letters on line 1.

Vowel Review

Practice these vowels by saying the sound of each and, if you know it, its name.

Practice these vowels in some easy words.

Vowel Color Coding

Color the vowels that say "ah" in "AQUA."
Color the vowels that say "eh" in "RED."
Color the vowels that say "ee" in "GREEN."
Color the vowels that say "oh" in "YELLOW."
Color the vowels that say "oo" in "BLUE."
The almost silent vowel gets no color.

Big Practice

Practice these words in Alef-Bet order.

1.	**א** אָדָם	**ב** בַּיִת	**ג** גֶּשֶׁם	**ד** דֹב	**ה** הַבְדָּלָה

2.	**ו** וַשְׁתִּי	**ז** זָהָב	**ח** חֹשֶׁן	**ט** טֶבַע	**י** יִשְׂרָאֵל

3.	**כ** כֹּתֶל	**ל** לוּחַ	**מ** מַצָּה	**נ** נֵר	**ס** סְבִיבוֹן

4.	**ע** עֵץ	**פ** פְּרִי	**צ** צֶדֶק	**ק** קָטָן	**ר** רֹאשׁ

5.	**שׁ** שׁוֹפָר	**שׂ** שִׂמְחָה	**ת** תּוֹרָה

Final Letters

Five letters have alternate forms called **סוֹפִית**, or ending.

Do you remember what each of these **סוֹפִית** says?

ד ם ן ף ץ

fa

Match each letter to its **סוֹפִית** version.

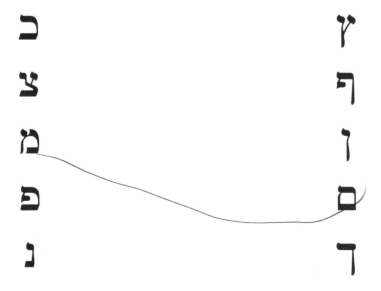

כ	ץ
צ	ף
מ	ן
פ	ם
נ	ד

Open the door. You come out of the cave and find yourself in the desert. Take as many camels for your journey as you need, as long as you can successfully complete these words. Add in the correct version of the letter in the box to complete the word.

Here are the beginning letters you will need to fill in the missing letters on page 31, line 8.

Sound-Alike Letters

Practice these words that have sound-alike letters.

וּמְסַדֵּר נְסַפֵּר שָׂשׂוֹן חֶסֶד שִׂמְחָה	שׂ and ס	.1
סְבִיבוֹן יִשְׂרָאֵל סוֹמֵךְ מַעֲשֶׂה סִדּוּר		.2
אֱמֶת עוֹשֶׂה עַתָּה אַתָּה אֶת עֵת	ע and א	.3
אֱלֹהֶיךָ לְמַעַן וְנֶאֱמַר אוֹהֵב בְּעַמּוֹ		.4
תָּשִׂים בְּטֶרֶם תְּהִלָּה הַתּוֹרָה וְטוֹב	ט and ת	.5
לְטֹטָפֹת וְשִׁנַּנְתָּם יִשְׁתַּבַּח תָּמִיד		.6
לִכְבוֹדוֹ בְּחֶסֶד כָּמֹכָה חַיִּים בָּרְכוּ	ח and כ	.7
בְּרַחֲמִים הַכּוֹכָבִים מַלְכוּתוֹ אֲנַחְנוּ		.8
בָּרָקִיעַ וְקוֹנֵה כֻּלָּם כָּמֹכָה קָדוֹשׁ	ק and כ	.9
מְקַדֵּשׁ מְכַלְכֵּל חֻקִּים כִּרְצוֹנוֹ		.10
אָבוֹת וְאָהַבְתָּ לֵב נָבִיא וָעֶד	ב and ו	.11
וְדִבַּרְתָּ וְנִשְׁמַח בָּנָיו הַבְדָּלָה		.12

10

You arrive at a well that is guarded by laser beams. In order to turn the laser beams off, you need to cut the right wires. Connect the sound-alike letters so you'll know which wires to cut. Mark the connections by over-lining each correct connection. Remember: If a letter has no sound-alike match, do not cut the wire or we'll all be dead...........

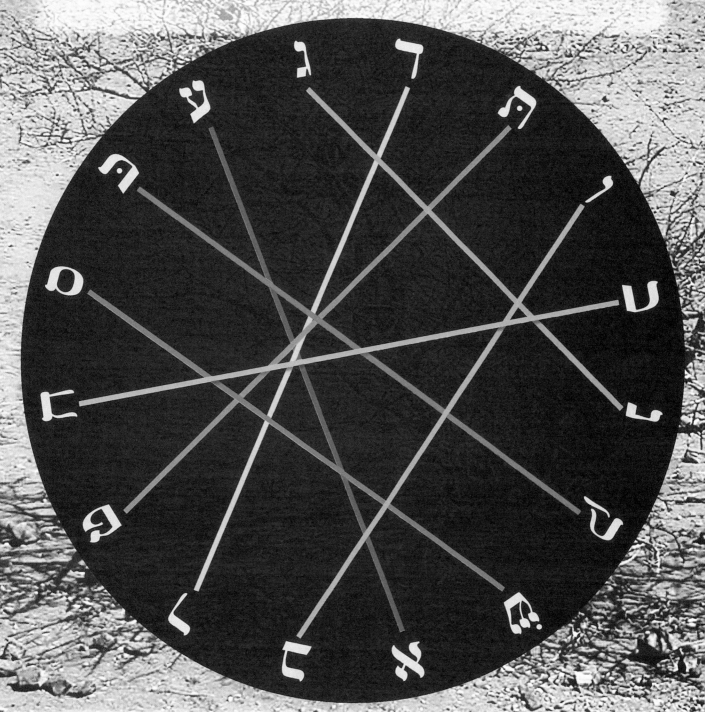

Go to page 31 and fill in the missing sound-alike letters on line 12.

Look-Alike Letters

Practice these words with the look-alike letters כ, בּ, בּ and כּ.

1. בָּרוּךְ בָּרְכוּ וְאָהַבְתָּ וּכְתַבְתָּם כָּמֹכָה

2. בְּשִׁבְתְּךָ וּבְלֶכְתְּךָ וּבְשָׁכְבְּךָ הַמְבֹרָךְ אַהֲבָה

Practice these words with the look-alike letters גּ and נ.

3. גּוֹלֵל מִפְּנֵי חֲנֻכָּה הַגֶּפֶן וְהִגִּיעָנוּ גְּוִיָּתִי

4. הַגָּדוֹל הַגִּבּוֹר וְהַנּוֹרָא שֶׁהֶחֱיָנוּ

Match these words with the look-alike letters ה, ח or ת\תּ
that either begin or appear in these word.

תּוֹרָה		וְנֶחְמָד
	ה	
חַיִּים		יְהוּדָה
הַלְלוּ		רַחֲמָן
	ת\תּ	
הָיְתָה		מְהֵרָה
חוֹלִי		מְחַדֵּשׁ
	ח	
תִּשְׁבְּחָן		בְּשִׁבְתְּךָ

You can hear grumbling coming from your camels and you know you must find them food. You come to a vending machine and, amazingly, it features "Camel Chips!" You get in line and when it's your turn, you push the buttons but nothing happens. Your camels are impatient. You must do something. You take a deep breath and focus all your attention on the task at hand... You finally notice the instructions.

Go to page 31 and find the clue word on line 2. Come back here and punch in that three-letter word.

It's a Family Affair

	Practice these words with the family letters **בּ** and **ב**.	שָׁכַב	כָּבוֹד	כּוֹכָב	כֶּלֶב	.1
		כָּמוֹךָ	מֶלֶךְ	כְּמִכָה	כָּמֹכָה	.2
		כְּמַלְכֵּנוּ	וּבְשָׁכְבְּךָ	וּבְלֶכְתְּךָ		.3

בּוֹא	אֶבֶן	בָּם	לֵב	בָּרָא	.4	Now practice these words with the family letters **בּ** and **ב**.
כָּבֵד	בָּרוּךְ	הַמְבֹרָךְ	בּוֹרֵא	.5	
אָבִינוּ	אַהֲבָה	יוֹשְׁבֵי	בָּרְכוּ	.6	

	Now try these words with the family letters **פּ** and **פ**.	עוֹף	אֵיפֹה	פּוּרִים	סֵפֶר	פִּיל	.7
		שׁוֹפָר	אָלֶף	פָּתְחוּ	כָּפָּה	.8
		מוּסָף	לִפְנֵי	מִפְּנֵי	תְּפִלָּה	.9

נָשִׁים	נָשִׁים	שָׂר	שַׂר	שָׂר	.10	Believe it or not, **שׂ** and **שׁ** are also family letters. Practice these words.
שִׂמְחָה	שָׂשׂוֹן	שָׁלֹשׁ	יִשְׂרָאֵל	.11	
שָׁלוֹם	עוֹשֶׂה	שְׂרִירָה	שְׂרִיטָה	.12	

14

The letters lead to the edge of a thick palm jungle. Walking through appears impossible. Then you notice that if you follow the path of letter families, you should be able to reach the other side safely. One wrong step will lose you in the depths of the jungle. You look carefully into the thicket and decide to begin at the letter בּ.

You reach the other side of the jungle safely. Go to page 31 and add the missing family letters (בּ or כּ) on line 16.

The ◌ְ Sh'va

This vowel ◌ְ is called the sh'va. It is a very interesting vowel because it does three different things.

1. When the ◌ְ is under the first letter of a word it makes the sound like the "ŏ" in the word "about."

2. Almost always, when the ◌ְ isn't under the first letter in a word, it has no sound. What the ◌ְ does then is end a word part. Usually the letter and the vowel before it combine with it to make up this word part.

3. Sometimes you will find two ◌ְ together. When you do, the first one is silent (and ends a word part) and the second one sounds like a ◌ְ under the first letter.

Sounding Clues

• Whether it is silent or not, a ◌ְ usually ends a word part.

• Sometimes the ◌ְ is combined with another vowel under one letter. Here it "shortens" the sound of the other vowel. Most of the time you won't notice.

Dividing Into Parts

Look at this familiar prayer. What does the ◌ְ tell us about dividing words into sayable parts?

בָּ/רְ/כוּ אֶת-יְיָ הַ/מְ/בֹ/רָךְ

בָּ/רוּךְ יְיָ הַ/מְ/בֹ/רָךְ לְ/עוֹ/לָם וָ/עֶד

Say these words aloud to help you divide them into parts.

מַלְכוּתוֹ בְּרָכוֹת יִשְׂרָאֵל שְׁמַע

מְבָרֵךְ לְעוֹלָם וְאִמְרוּ מְלֹא

16

You follow the trail of Deke Duke to the river. You notice that there are word parts on the river banks. Divide these words and fill in the word pieces on each side of the river. Then cross the river to follow Deke's trail.

4. אַשְׁרֵי   3. וָעֶד   2. פְּתָחוּ   1. שְׁמַע

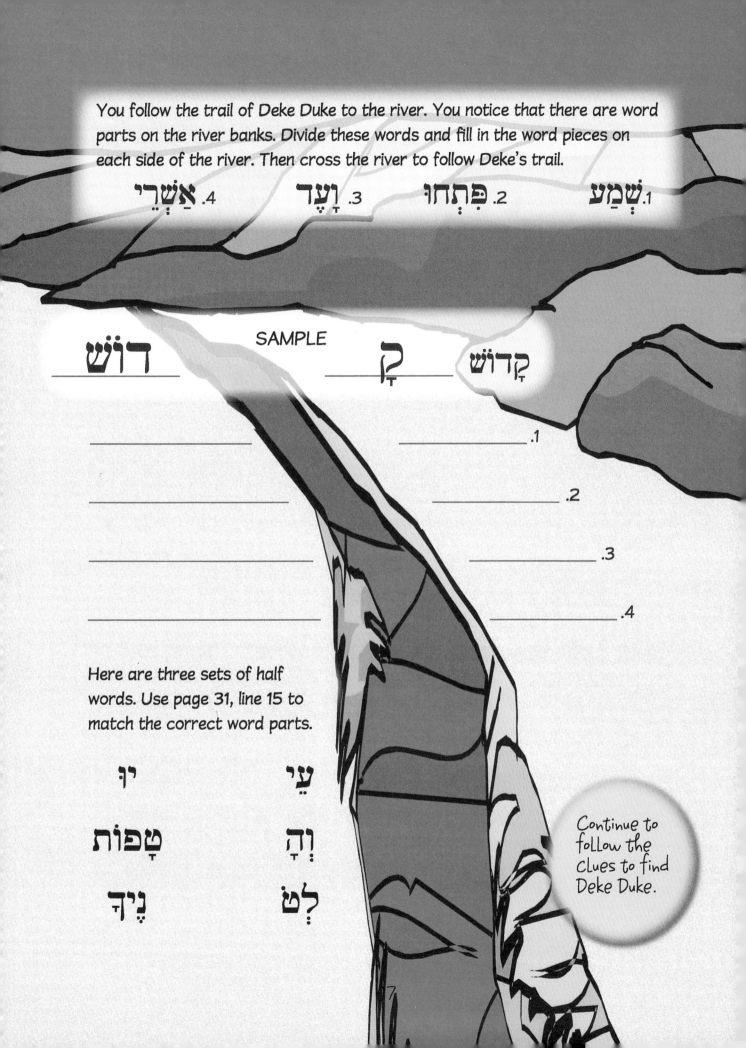

SAMPLE

דוֹשׁ   קְ   קָדוֹשׁ

_____   _____ .1

_____   _____ .2

_____   _____ .3

_____   _____ .4

Here are three sets of half words. Use page 31, line 15 to match the correct word parts.

עֵי   יוֹ

וְהָ   טָפוֹת

לִטֹ   נֶיךָ

Continue to follow the clues to find Deke Duke.

7

Special Vowels

Kammatz Katan

Sometimes the vowel ◼ is pronounced like an וֹ and not an ◼. It is called a kammatz katan. In many books the kammatz katan is printed a little larger than an ordinary ◼ kammatz. It makes it easier for you to recognize it.

Kammatz katan means "short kammatz." A regular ◼ makes an "ah" sound. A ◼ makes an "awe" sound. According to people who study languages, "awe" is a short "ah".

Hataf Vowels

Sometimes the ◼ is combined with another vowel under one letter. Here it "shortens" the sound of the other vowel.

The ◼ can be combined with a segol to become a ◼ hataf segol, and with a ◼ pataẖ to become a ◼ hataf pataẖ. The ◼ doesn't change the sound, so ◼ = ◼ and ◼ = ◼.

The ◼ hataf kammatz is pronounced "awe." It is also a "short kammatz." It is not found in many words.

Practice these phrases from the Siddur. Hightlight every word that has a ◼ in orange, a ◼ in blue, and a ◼ in green.

1. קָדוֹשׁ קָדוֹשׁ קָדוֹשׁ יי צְבָאוֹת מְלֹא כָל־הָאָרֶץ כְּבוֹדוֹ

2. וְאָהַבְתָּ אֵת יי אֱלֹהֶיךָ בְּכָל־לְבָבְךָ וּבְכָל־נַפְשְׁךָ וּבְכָל־מְאֹדֶךָ

3. וְתֶחֱזֶינָה עֵינֵינוּ בְּשׁוּבְךָ לְצִיּוֹן בְּרַחֲמִים

4. שֶׁהֶחֱיָנוּ וְקִיְּמָנוּ וְהִגִּיעָנוּ לַזְּמַן הַזֶּה

5. בָּרוּךְ אַתָּה יי אֱלֹהֵינוּ וֵאלֹהֵי אֲבוֹתֵינוּ וְאִמּוֹתֵינוּ.

6. אֱלֹהִים, בְּרָב חַסְדֶּךָ, עֲנֵנִי בֶּאֱמֶת יִשְׁעֶךָ

אֱלֹהֶיךָ

וְאָהַבְתָּ

בְּרַחֲמִים

חַסְדֶּךָ

שֶׁהֶחֱיָנוּ

נַפְשֶׁךָ

בְּרֹב

יִשְׁעֶךָ

וֵאלֹהֵי

בֶּאֱמֶת

וְתֶחֱזֶינָה

קָדוֹשׁ

כְּבוֹדוֹ

וּבְכָל

You see a speedboat and you know that Deke is on it. Grab the boat at the dock below and follow him by saying all the words in your path.

Now go to page 31, line 13 and put in the special vowel *kammatz katan.*

Two Roots

Almost all Hebrew words are built from three-letter roots. Here are two to study.

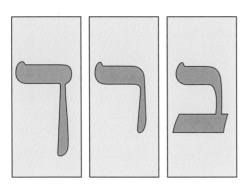

הַמְבֹרָךְ   בָּרְכוּ   בָּרוּךְ

blessed = בָּרוּךְ

bless (plural) = בָּרְכוּ

the One Who is blessed = הַמְבֹרָךְ

Practice these ברך words.

1. בָּרוּךְ   בָּרְכוּ   מְבֹרָךְ   מְבָרֵךְ   בֵּרֵךְ   בִּרְכַּת

קִדְּשָׁנוּ   מְקַדֵּשׁ   קָדוֹשׁ

Holy = קָדוֹשׁ

makes Holy = מְקַדֵּשׁ

He made us Holy = קִדְּשָׁנוּ

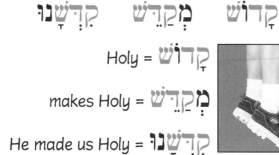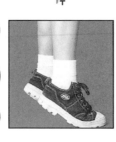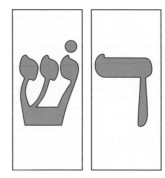

Practice these קדשׁ words.

2. קָדוֹשׁ   מְקַדֵּשׁ   קְדוֹשִׁים   שֶׁמְּקַדִּישִׁים   וְתִתְקַדֵּשׁ   נְקַדֵּשׁ

Write in the missing letters for these words built from the roots קָדוֹשׁ and בּרך.

7. בָּרְ____וּ   5. ____רוּכִים   3. ____דוֹשׁ

8. הַמְ____רָךְ   6. קָ____וֹשׁ   4. מְקַדֵּ____

20

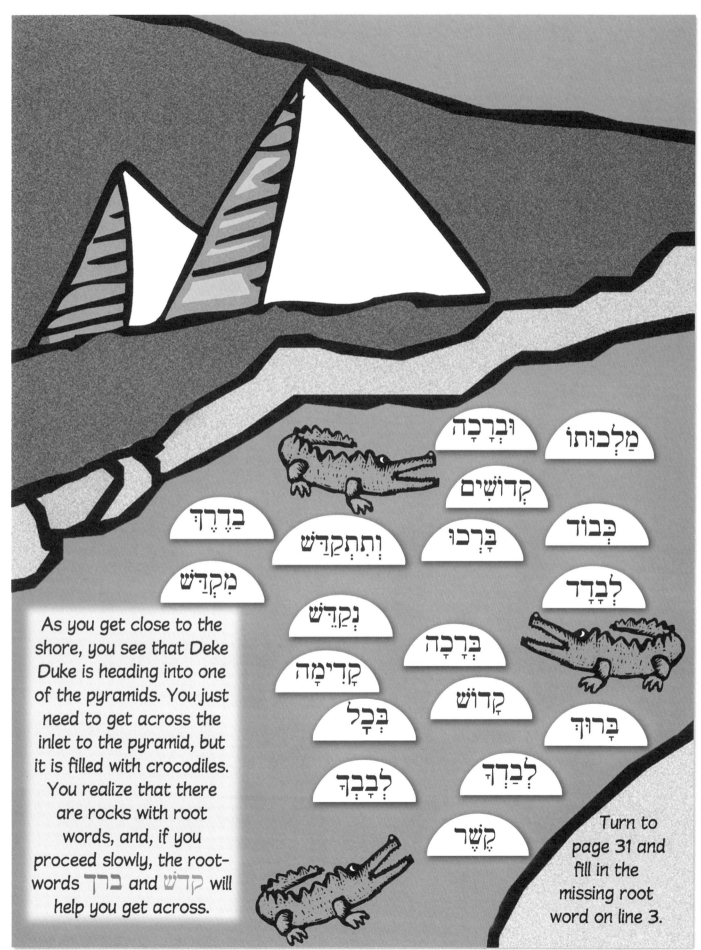

As you get close to the shore, you see that Deke Duke is heading into one of the pyramids. You just need to get across the inlet to the pyramid, but it is filled with crocodiles. You realize that there are rocks with root words, and, if you proceed slowly, the root-words ברך and קדש will help you get across.

מַלְכוּתוֹ

וּבְרָכָה

קְדוֹשִׁים

כָּבוֹד

בָּרְכוּ

בַּדֶּרֶךְ

וְתִתְקַדַּשׁ

לְבַדָד

מִקְדַּשׁ

נְקַדֵּשׁ

בְּרָכָה

קָדִימָה

קָדוֹשׁ

בְּכָל

בָּרוּךְ

לְבַדֶךָ

לִבָבֶךָ

קֶשֶׁר

Turn to page 31 and fill in the missing root word on line 3.

Beginnings

Some words have parts added to the beginning called prefixes. Here are some common prefixes.

לְהוֹדוֹת
TO give thanks

בְּבֵיתֶךָ
IN your house

וְאָהַבְתָּ
AND you shall love

הָעֵץ
THE tree

Practice these words and circle the prefixes.

1. לְעוֹלָם הַכֹּל בְּיוֹם וְעַל לְבַדּוֹ הָעֵץ וְתֶן

2. בְּעַמּוֹ וְלָשׁוֹן בְּאַהֲבָה הַזֶּה הָאָרֶץ לְדַבֵּר

Endings

Some words have parts added to the end called suffixes. Here are some common suffixes.

עֵינֵינוּ
OUR eyes

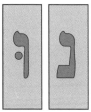

בְּתוֹרָתֶךָ
in YOUR Torah

Practice these words and circle the suffixes.

3. אֱלֹהֵינוּ אֱלֹהֶיךָ אֲדוֹנֵינוּ לְבָבְךָ לְבֶךָ בְּטֶחָנוּ

4. לִבֵּנוּ שְׁמֶךָ קִדַּשְׁנוּ בְּתוֹרָתֶךָ לְבָבֵנוּ לְבָנֶיךָ

As you reach dry land, you bump into noted Egyptologist Radcliff Emerson. He has just seen Deke Duke go into the big pyramid. As you begin to creep forward, Professor Emerson screams, "Watch out for the charging rhinoceros!" To get past the rhino read these words that have both a prefix and a suffix.

Once you've are past the rhino, Go to page 31 and fill in the missing prefixes and suffixes on line 9.

בְּתוֹרָתֶךָ

וְאַהֲבָתְךָ

בְּחַסְדְּךָ

לְבָנֶיךָ

בְּעֵינֵינוּ

וְהַצִּילֵנוּ   בְּמִצְוֹתֶיךָ

23

The Double-Duty Dot
מֹשֶׁה

Look at the name above. How would you read it?

If you guessed "Moshe," you would be correct.

When you have an "◼" vowel and a שׁ following it, one of the dots drops out. The one that remains is both the dot for the vowel ◼ and the dot for the שׁ. It is called the double-duty dot.

Practice these words. Circle the words with the double-duty dot.

1. הַמְבֹרָךְ   חֹשֶׁן   כָּמֹכָה   חֹשֶׁךְ   שְׁלֹשָׁה   עֹשֶׂה

The Dagesh

בּ ב כּ כ פּ פ

A. Name these Hebrew letters: בּ ב כּ כ פּ פ

B. The dot found inside פּ, בּ, and כּ is called a *dagesh*. What does the *dagesh* do to these letters?

C. The *dagesh* can also be found in most other Hebrew letters, but in these letters it doesn't change the way each letter is pronounced. It changes the grammar of the word, but not really the sound.

Circle the letter whose sound is changed by the *dagesh*.

דּ   לּ   מּ   גּ   בּ   תּ   שּׁ   פּ   זּ   כּ

D. Now practice these words with a *dagesh*. Circle the words that have letter that changes its sound.

2. בָּרְכוּ   דִּבַּרְתָּ   תְּפִלָּה   הַגֶּפֶן   גּוֹלֵל   מַצָּה   עַמּוֹ

3. חַיִּים   כְּבוֹדוֹ   פְּנֵי   מִקְדָּשׁ   כֹּל   מְכַלְכֵּל

24

Before entering the pyramid you come across a sign that says "Dot-Sniffing Dogs Rented Here." Abdallah tells you to buy the dog who can tell the dagesh that changes the sound of the letter. You decide to the best dog for you has the double-duty dot. Circle your choice!

פַּרְעֹה   מֹשֶׁה   יַעֲקֹב

Enter the pyramid and follow the words with a dagesh that changes the sound of the letter (the hieroglyphs on the wall will point the way). By the way, watch out for the mystical eye. It guards the secret chamber and will send you falling straight to the bottom in darkness.

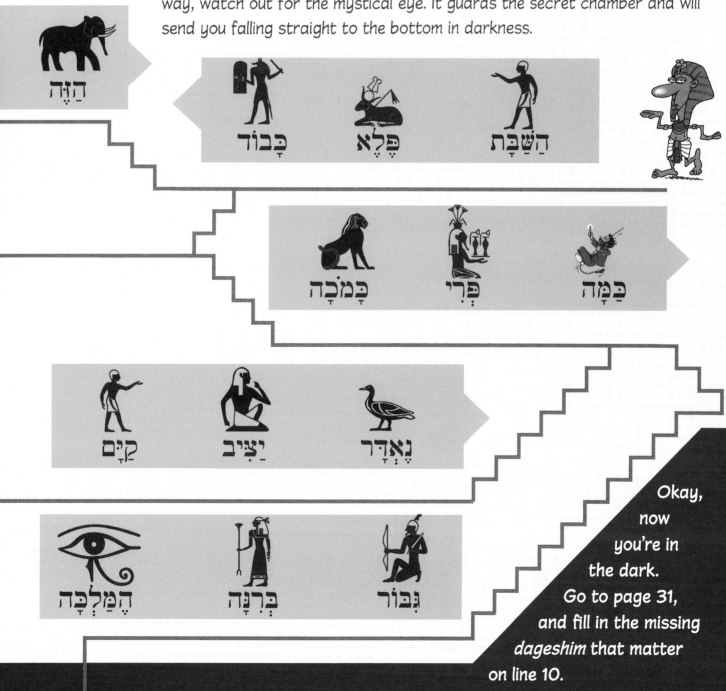

הַזֶּה

כָּבוֹד   פֶּלֶא   הַשַׁבָּת

כָּמֹכָה   פְּרִי   כַּמָּה

קָיָם   יַצִּיב   נֶאְדָּר

הַמַּלְכָּה   בְּרָנָּה   גִּבּוֹר

Okay, now you're in the dark. Go to page 31, and fill in the missing *dageshim* that matter on line 10.

The Very Confusing Letter וֹ

The letter ו can be very complicated. Sometimes it makes the sound of a letter, sometimes the sound of a vowel and sometimes it makes both.

In most cases: • ו says "v," as in וְאָהַבְתָּ.

• וֹ says "oh," as in שָׁלוֹם.

• וּ says "oo," as in בָּרוּךְ.

except when: • וֹ says "voh," as in בְּמִצְוֹתָיו (the ו and וֹ merge).

• וּ says "v," as in וְצִוָּנוּ (the ו has a dagesh in it).

The וּ (ו with a dagesh) and the וֹ that makes the sound of both the letter and the vowel are very confusing. The BIG TRICK to remembering these two funny ו combinations is:

CLUE: IN HEBREW YOU WILL ALMOST NEVER FIND
TWO VOWELS IN A ROW WITHOUT
A LETTER (CONSONANT) IN BETWEEN.

Take מִצְוֹת, for example. Since there is a ▪ (sh'va) under the צ, the וֹ cannot be a vowel because the ▪ and וֹ would make two vowels in a row. In this case the וֹ is both a ו that says "v" and a וֹ that says "oh."

Try out these words. Circle the words that have a וֹ that is both a ו and a וֹ. Draw a box around the words that have a וּ that is only a ו with a dagesh.

1. צַוֶּה בְּמִצְוֹתָיו כַּוֵּן מַלְכוּתוֹ וְצִוָּנוּ

2. כֹּל כַּוָּנָה עִוֵּר מָזוֹן שָׁוֵּו מִצְוֶה

3. מִצְוֹת תִּקְוָה מִצְוֹת כַּכָּתוּב וְדִבַּרְתָּ

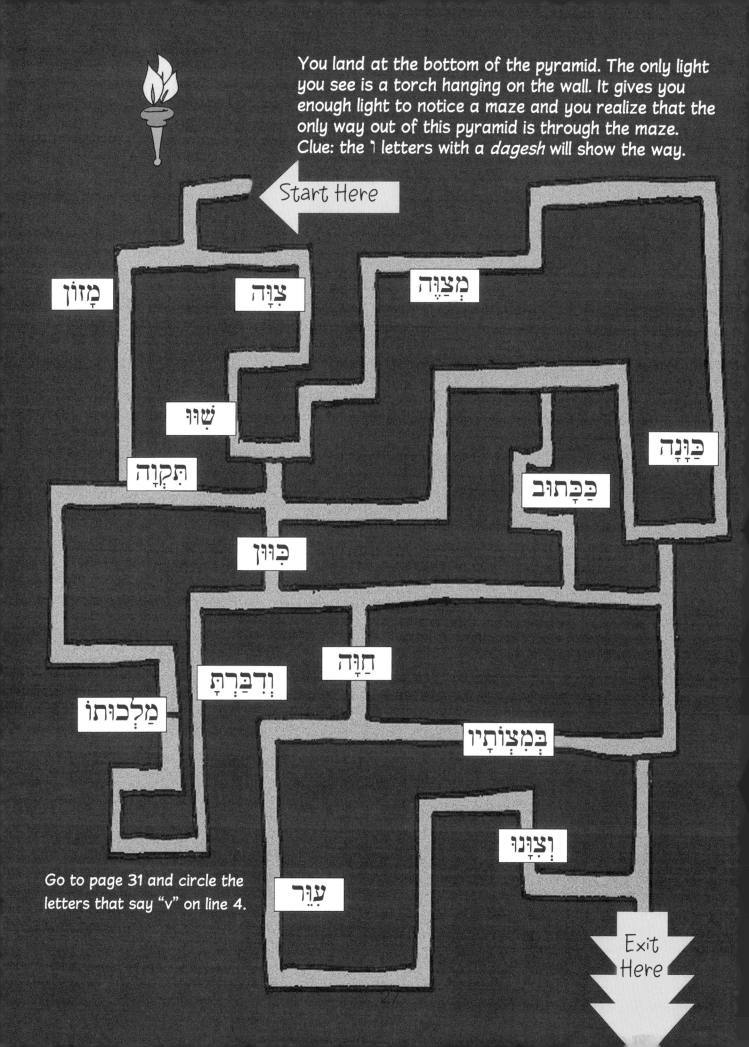

You land at the bottom of the pyramid. The only light you see is a torch hanging on the wall. It gives you enough light to notice a maze and you realize that the only way out of this pyramid is through the maze. Clue: the ו letters with a *dagesh* will show the way.

Start Here

מָזוֹן

צַוָּה

מִצְוָה

שָׁוֶּוּ

כּוֹנֵה

תִּקְוָה

כַּכָּתוּב

כִּוֵן

וְדִבַּרְתָּ

חַוָּה

מַלְכוּתוֹ

בְּמִצְוֹתָיו

Go to page 31 and circle the letters that say "v" on line 4.

עִוֵּר

וְצִוָּנוּ

Exit Here

More About Final Letters

Practice these words and phrases that have סוֹפִית letters.

מֶלֶךְ חֹשֶׁךְ יָדֶיךָ שְׁמֶךָ מַלְאָךְ	ךְ	1.
בְּכָל־לְבָבְךָ וּבְכָל־נַפְשְׁךָ וּבְכָל־מְאֹדֶךָ.		2.
שֵׁם כֻּלָּם וְשִׁנַּנְתָּם הַמְּלָכִים	ם	3.
וְשִׁנַּנְתָּם לְבָנֶיךָ וְדִבַּרְתָּ בָּם		4.
גֶּפֶן לָשׁוֹן נָכוֹן רָצוֹן זִכָּרוֹן	ן	5.
אֵין כֵּאלֹהֵינוּ, אֵין כַּאדוֹנֵינוּ, אֵין כְּמַלְכֵּנוּ		6.
עָיֵף קוֹף סוֹף לְהִתְעַטֵּף מוּסָף	ף	7.
סוֹף מַעֲשֶׂה בְּמַחֲשָׁבָה תְּחִלָּה		8.
לָרוּץ אָמֵץ חָלוּץ מֵלִיץ אֶרֶץ	ץ	9.
הַמּוֹצִיא לֶחֶם מִן הָאָרֶץ		10.

28

You find your way out of the pyramid and see Deke taking off in a plane. You see that another plane is getting ready for flight. You catch the pilot in time. He asks to see your ticket. You find a ticket in your pocket and give it to him. He frowns and reports that important information is missing from the ticket. You sit **down to quickly add the missing family letters.**

TO VALIDATE THIS TICKET WRITE THE MISSING LETTERS TO COMPLETE THE PATTERN

Now jump in the plane and get going or you will miss Deke. But first add in all the missing final letters on page 31, line 6.

Missing Word Challenge

Here are seven Siddur phrases. Deke Duke has removed one word from each phrase. Write in the missing word for each phrase (see the answers below.

1. יִשְׂרָאֵל יי אֱלֹהֵינוּ יי אֶחָד _____

2. בָּרְכוּ אֶת־יי _____

3. מִי־ _____ בָּאֵלִים יי

4. קָדוֹשׁ _____ קָדוֹשׁ יי צְבָאוֹת

5. עֹשֶׂה _____ בִּמְרוֹמָיו

6. שֶׁהֶחֱיָנוּ וְקִיְּמָנוּ וְהִגִּיעָנוּ לַזְּמַן _____

7. _____ אֵת יי אֱלֹהֶיךָ

Go to page 31 and write in the missing word on line 1. It is the name of the prayer.

Answers

קָדוֹשׁ   הַזֶּה   הַמְבֹרָךְ

שָׁלוֹם   שְׁמַע   כָּמֹכָה   וְאָהַבְתָּ

שְׁמַע וְאָהַבְתָּ

1. _____ △◯□

2. יי אֱלֹהֵינוּ יי אֶחָד.

3. ___ ___ ___וּ שֵׁם כְּבוֹד מַלְכוּתוֹ

4. לְעוֹלָם וָעֶד.

5. וְאָהַבְתָּ אֵת יי אֱלֹהֶיךָ

6. בְּכָל-לְבָבְךָ · וּבְכָל-נַפְשְׁךָ · וּבְכָל-מְאֹדֶךָ ··.

7. וְהָיוּ הַדְּבָרִים הָאֵלֶה

(remember, right to left)

8. אֲשֶׁר אָנֹ·י מְצַוְּךָ הַיּוֹם עַל לְבָבֶךָ .

9. ··. שִׁנַּנְתָּם ·· בְּנֶי ·ךָ

10. וְדִבַּרְתָּ בָּם

(Add in the missing dagesh)

11. בְּשִׁבְתְּךָ בְּבֵיתֶךָ

12. וּ·בְלֶ·כְתְּךָ בַ·דֶּרֶךְ

*(Clue: It **sounds** like וּבְלֶכְתְּךָ וַדֶּרֶךְ)*

13. וּבְשָׁכְבְּךָ וּבְקוּמֶךָ

(Add in the missing kammatz katan)

14. וּקְשַׁרְתָּם לְ_____ עַל-יָדֶךָ

(אוֹר or אוֹת)

15. וְהָיוּ לְטֹטָפוֹת בֵּין עֵינֶיךָ.

16. וּכְתַ·בְתָּם עַל-מְזֻזוֹת ·· בֵּיתֶךָ וּ·בִשְׁעָרֶיךָ.

(ב or בּ)

Now that you've filled in all the missing elements, practice the complete שְׁמַע וְאָהַבְתָּ.

31

Your plane is following Deke Duke's plane. All of a sudden he jumps from the plane. You can see in his right hand the silver Yad with the ruby on the end. As he falls through the air, he grabs at his rip cord and his parachute opens. You grab your chute and jump out of your plane after him.

You put on the chute as you fall, then move into a skydiving position. You fall as far as you can, landing right next to Deke Duke's deflated parachute. He has landed in muddy soil, and you follow his foot prints. When he hits the sidewalk, his footprints are still easy to follow. He runs into a building and you are hot on his trail. He runs up six flights of stairs and goes out onto the roof. You open the door to the roof just as Deke Duke takes off in a helicopter.

You see a metal box on the roof. Attached is a note that says: "You are way too much for me. I need some rest. The Yad is in this box. All you have to do to open it is read the whole text on page 31. Good luck. By the way, your synagogue has a nice Torah breastplate!"